Farm Fun

Farm Buildings

by Tessa Kenan

Bullfrog Books

Ideas for Parents and Teachers

Bullfrog Books let children practice reading informational text at the earliest reading levels. Repetition, familiar words, and photo labels support early readers.

Before Reading

- Discuss the cover photo. What does it tell them?
- Look at the picture glossary together. Read and discuss the words.

Read the Book

- "Walk" through the book and look at the photos. Let the child ask questions. Point out the photo labels.
- Read the book to the child, or have him or her read independently.

After Reading

- Prompt the child to think more. Ask: Have you seen a farm before? What buildings did you see?

Bullfrog Books are published by Jump!
5357 Penn Avenue South
Minneapolis, MN 55419
www.jumplibrary.com

Library of Congress Cataloging-in-Publication Data

Names: Kenan, Tessa, author.
Title: Farm buildings / Tessa Kenan.
Description: Minneapolis: Jump!, Inc., 2021.
Series: Farm fun | Includes index.
Audience: Ages 5–8 | Audience: Grades K–1
Identifiers: LCCN 2019053384 (print)
LCCN 2019053385 (ebook)
ISBN 9781645275213 (hardcover)
ISBN 9781645275220 (ebook)
Subjects: LCSH: Farm buildings—Juvenile literature.
Classification: LCC S782 .K46 2021 (print)
LCC S782 (ebook) | DDC 631.2—dc23
LC record available at https://lccn.loc.gov/2019053384
LC ebook record available at https://lccn.locgov/2019053385

Editor: Jenna Gleisner
Designer: David Stavitzski

Photo Credits: benedek/iStock, cover; Mint Images/Getty, 1; travelview/Shutterstock, 3; Peter Kim/Shutterstock, 4, 22; Ron and Patty Thomas/iStock, 5; 1968/Shutterstock, 6–7, 22; Wayne Mckown/Dreamstime, 8–9, 23tr; SimplyCreativePhotography/iStock, 10, 22; Fascinadora/iStock, 11, 22, 23tl; Gary Crabbe/age fotostock/SuperStock, 12–13, 22; NicolasMcComber/iStock, 14–15; Maxym022/Dreamstime, 16, 22; stefan11/Shutterstock, 17, 22; Tennesseewitney/Dreamstime, 18–19; Ridofranz/Getty, 20–21 (foreground); davelogan/iStock, 20–21 (background); effective stock photos/Shutterstock, 23bl; Artazum/Shutterstock, 23br; mihaiulia/Shutterstock, 24.

Printed in the United States of America at Corporate Graphics in North Mankato, Minnesota.

Table of Contents

Many Buildings

What is this building?

A barn!

It is just one farm building.
There are many.
Let's take a look!

Barns are big.

Cows live in this one.

They stay safe
and warm inside.

Cows eat hay.

Yum!

Hay is stored in the hayloft.

hayloft
hay

Silos store grain.
They are tall.

They keep grain dry.

The coop is small.
It is where chickens live!

coop
chickens

stall

This is a horse stable.
Horses live in stalls.

Machines go in this shed.
Like what?

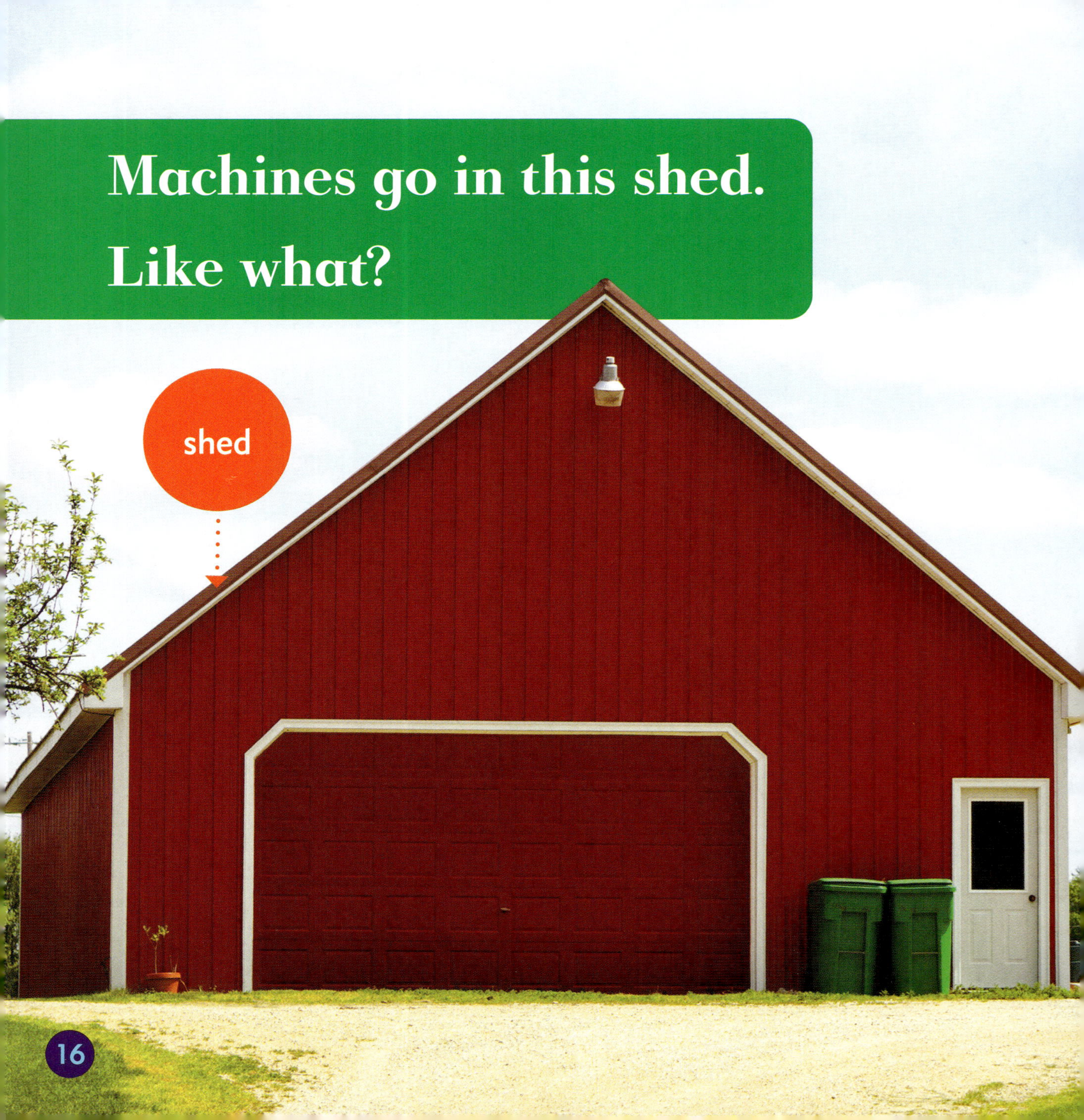

Tractors!

A farmer has many tools.

He keeps them in his workshop.

Cool!

There are many buildings on a farm.

The farmer lives in the farmhouse!

Do you want to visit?

What Goes Where?

Farm buildings protect what is inside them. Point to the building each item goes in.

Picture Glossary

grain
Small, hard seeds that are harvested.

hay
Long grass that is dried and used as food for farm animals.

hayloft
A platform high above the floor of a barn where hay is stored.

stable
A building or a part of a building where horses are fed and housed.

Index

To Learn More

Finding more information is as easy as 1, 2, 3.

1. Go to www.factsurfer.com
2. Enter "farmbuildings" into the search box.
3. Click the "Surf" button to see a list of websites.